Hide and Seek

by Lynne Rickards
illustrated by Moni Perez

Zara liked feeding the baby chicks. She liked to fill up their dish and watch them peck.

'One, two, three chicks,' said Zara.
'Fluff, Puff and Scruff.'

One day the cage door was open.
Zara looked inside.

One, two ... wait! Where was Scruff?

'Miss Garcia!' called Zara. 'Scruff is gone! We have to find her!'

All the children jumped up to help. Miss Garcia told them where to look.

Omar and Beno looked on the floor.

Zara and Leila looked on shelves and tables. Kofi looked under Miss Garcia's desk.

Everyone was talking as they looked.
Where was Scruff? How did she get out?

'Shh, class!' said Miss Garcia. 'I can hear a noise. Let's listen.'

All the children stood still. *Scratch, scratch.*
There **was** a noise!

Scratch, scratch. There it was again!

The scratching was coming from the back of the classroom.

Scratch, scratch, scratch … peep, peep, peep!
'There she is!' said Miss Garcia.

'I think Scruff was playing Hide and Seek!'
said Zara.

Hide and Seek ☙ Lynne Rickards

Using this book

Developing reading comprehension

The story, set in a school, tells of three little chicks being looked after by the pupils. When the cage door is left open, they assume that the one of the chicks has escaped. After looking, the children discover that the chick had never left the cage after all.

The reader has to infer that the chick has not left the cage by the position of the environmental sounds at the back of the classroom. The relevance of the title 'Hide and Seek' becomes clear only at the end of the story. Teacher questioning to focus children on how we know that Scruff never left the cage will be helpful to support the development of inference skills.

Grammar and sentence structure

- Using speech marks and print details (bold print, for example) to inform reading with expression.
- Use of an abstract pronoun; *There was a noise; There she is; There it was again.*

Word meaning and spelling

- Synonyms for talking; *called, said* and their link to meaning.
- Decoding words with 3 letter consonant blends; *Scratch, Scruff, three.*

Curriculum links

Taking care of animals would link well with this book. Discussing how to care for animals properly, the importance of feeding and exercise routines and people who care for animals would all make helpful links with the story.

Science activities to understand life cycles and growth would also develop the storyline.

Learning Outcomes

Children can:

- read fluently with attention to punctuation
- discuss and interpret character
- solve new words using print detail while attending to meaning and syntax.

A guided reading lesson

Introducing the text

Give each child a copy of the book and read the title.

Orientation

Give a brief orientation to the text: *The children are looking after three little chicks; Fluff, Puff and Scruff. Every day they count them; One, two, three (pointing on the title page). Every day they feed them.*

Preparation

Make sure the children know the names of the children and the teacher in the story. If it is the first time they have read an International School story, show the children which child is which in the book.

page 2: Here is Zara, feeding the chicks. Where do they live?

page 3: Are all the chicks in the cage?

page 4: What has happened? How do you think it got out?

The children looked everywhere...

page 10: Miss Garcia has heard something – what do you think she has heard?

Let's read the story and find out.

Strategy Check

Prepare the children for the reading strategies required at Green band.

If you get stuck you can go back to the beginning of the line and think about what

Why Bird

written by Anne Giulieri

Engage Literacy is published in 2013 by Raintree.
Raintree is an imprint of Capstone Global Library Limited, a company
incorporated in Engand and Wales having its registered office at 7 Pilgrim
Street, London, EC4V 6LB – Registered company number: 6695582
www.raintreepublishers.co.uk

Originally published in Australia by Hinkler Education, a division
of Hinkler Books Pty Ltd.
Text copyright © Anne Giulieri 2012
Illustration copyright © Hinkler Books Pty Ltd 2012

Written by Anne Giulieri
Lead authors Jay Dale and Anne Giulieri
Illustrations on pp 17, 24 by Gaston Vanzet
Cover photography and photography on pp 4–15 by Ned Meldrum
Edited by Gwenda Smyth
UK edition edited by Dan Nunn, Catherine Veitch and Sian Smith
Designed by Susannah Low, Butterflyrocket Design

Whirly Bird
ISBN: 978 1 406 26509 5
10 9 8 7 6 5 4 3 2

Printed and bound in the United Kingdom.

Acknowledgements
p5 (and Contents page): © Paul Prescott | Dreamstime.com; p16 top:
© Expozer | Dreamstime.com; p16 middle (and back cover): © Mira
Agron | Dreamstime.com; p16 bottom: iStockphoto.com/ © Daniel Loiselle;
p18 middle: © Vevesoran | Dreamstime.com; p18 bottom: © Peter Lovás
| Dreamstime.com; p19: © Matthew Ragen | Dreamstime.com; p20:
© Snowball | Dreamstime.com; p21: © Manuel Hoo | Dreamstime.com;
p23 top left: © Gail Johnson | Dreamstime.com; p23 top right: © Bob Suir |
Dreamstime.com; p23 bottom (both): © Deyan Georgiev | Dreamstime.com

Contents

How to Make a Whirly Bird

Do you think you can make a piece
of paper or card *whirl* through the air?
You can! It's very easy to do.
This is how you do it.

All you need is a piece of paper or card,
a few cuts and some clever folding.
You'll be able to make an amazing
flying machine.

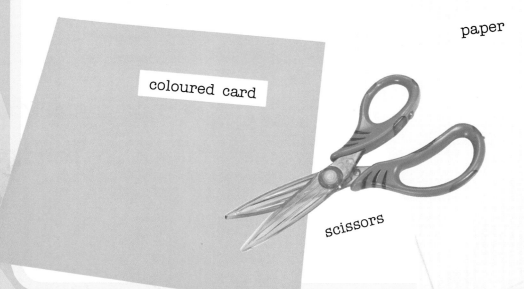

paper

coloured card

scissors

It's lots of fun to make.
It's called a whirly bird because it whirls
round and round like a *helicopter*.

First you need to get a piece of card.
Draw the folding lines
and the cutting lines on your card.
Make sure you take your time,
so that the fold and cut lines
are exactly where they should be.
It will look like this.

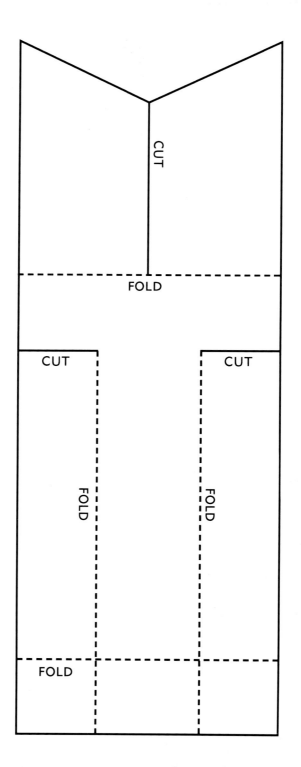

7

2

Now cut out
your whirly bird.

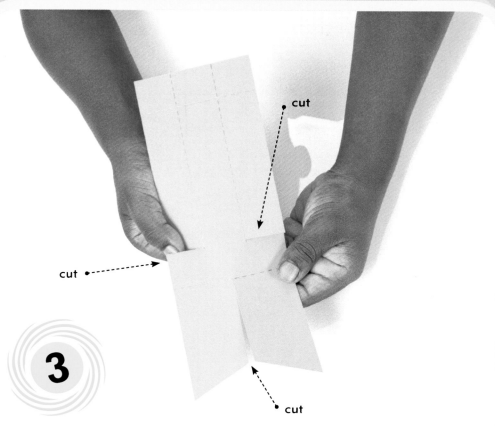

cut

cut

cut

3

Then cut your card along the cutting lines. There are three lines that you'll need to cut. One cutting line helps to make the *blades* and the other two cutting lines help to make the *shaft*.

Your card should look like this.

4

You are now ready to fold
the blades on your whirly bird.
Fold one part *forwards*
and one part *backwards*, like this.

This makes the blades of your whirly bird.
Your card should look like this.

5

You are now ready to fold
the shaft of your whirly bird.
Fold one side forwards
and the other side backwards, like this.

This helps to make a strong shaft
for the whirly bird.
It will now look like this.

6

The last thing you need to do
is to fold up the bottom of the shaft.
This helps the whirly bird to stay
in the air longer.
Your whirly bird will now look like this.

Your whirly bird is now complete
and ready to fly.
Hold it by the shaft, as high as you can,
and then let it go.
The blades will go round and round.
As it spins, it looks like a helicopter
coming down to land.

Helicopters and How They Work

Flying in Different Directions

Helicopters are amazing flying machines.
The word 'helicopter' means 'turning wing'.
The 'wings' on a helicopter are called
blades or *rotors*.
A helicopter is a *rotor-craft*.
It has large rotors
that turn round and round.

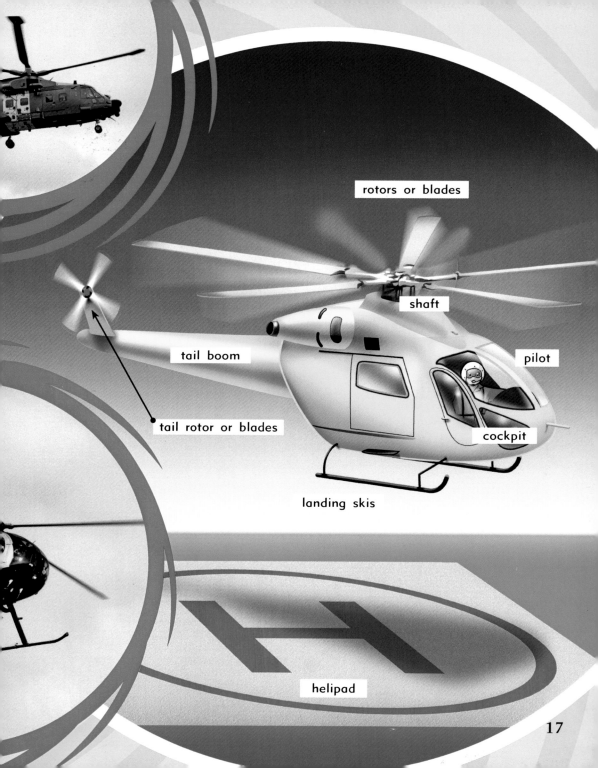

rotors or blades

shaft

tail boom

pilot

tail rotor or blades

cockpit

landing skis

helipad

17

Helicopters are special because
they can fly in many different ways.
The moving blades help the helicopter
to fly in all *directions*.

The moving blades help
the helicopter to take off.
When a helicopter takes off,
it goes straight up.
When a helicopter lands,
it goes straight down.

The moving blades help
the helicopter to fly.
It can go backwards,
forwards and sideways.
The moving blades also allow
the helicopter to hover.
This means it stays in one spot.

A helicopter moves in a special way.
This means it can fly in and out of places
that are hard for a plane to get to.

Helicopters do not need
a long *runway* as most planes do.
A helicopter needs just a small space
to land on.
The space doesn't need to be much
bigger than the helicopter itself.

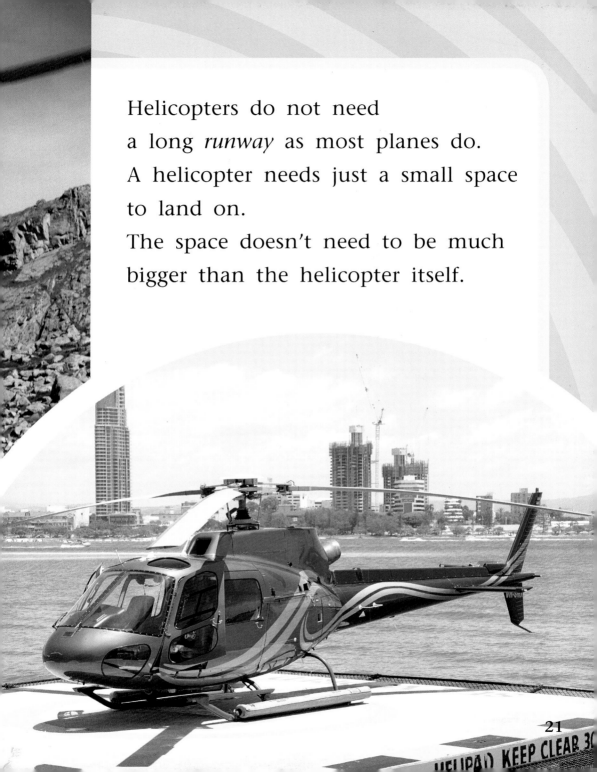

HELIPAD KEEP CLEAR 30

Useful Flying Machines

The special way in which helicopters can move makes them very useful flying machines.

Helicopters can be useful
in many different ways.
They can be used to transport (move) people or things.
They can be used to help fight fires by carrying large tanks of water.

They can also be used to save people who are lost at sea,
or people who are trapped
in hard-to-reach places.
So, as you can see, helicopters are really amazing flying machines!

Picture Glossary

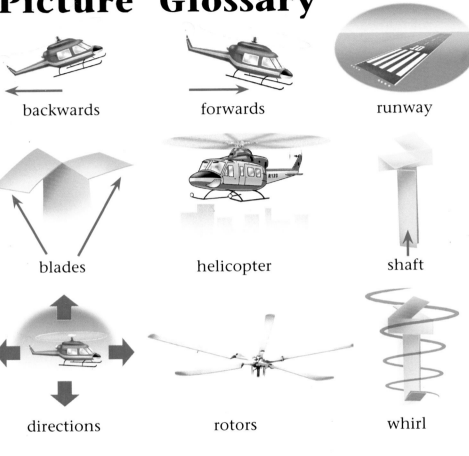

backwards

forwards

runway

blades

helicopter

shaft

directions

rotors

whirl

flying machine/s

rotor-craft

24